WELCOME TO THE NEW YEAR'S ENERGIES OF WATER TIGER 2022

The past year may have been incredibly challenging for you. Many countries have had to adapt to different ways of keeping their people safe and protected from the pandemic that has brought so much chaos to the world.

It is true to say that the world has been turned upside down with COVID-19!

The last year has been a genuine test of human spirit and one's strength of self.

We have all had to adjust our lifestyles to the new reality, adapting to different severities of lockdown, in different ways. How we adapted depended on where we lived, government policies, family dynamics how one was confined and the ability to revitalize and nourish one selves.

Can in this new reality, Feng Shui help?

Feng shui has no magic cure, however knowledge and placement using symbolic cures may help reduce vulnerability to current times.

2022 is the Year of Water Tiger. The coming year is dominated by this dynamic and charming creature. The Tiger - because of the sheer, raw power of the Tiger, is honored in China as the ultimate protector of home, family and health. The Tiger's warm hearted, sociable, and friendly. The year 2022 brings the lucky Tiger, which represents the greatest power on earth and is the emblem of protection for human life.

2022 Astrology & Feng Shui diary gives you the advantage of being prepared with daily insight into your health, harmony, love, and business opportunities. Providing you with tips for your home from Chinese Astrology, Flying Star and the school of Bagua.

Tune into the changes and energies you need to take into consideration during 2022.

- 2022 brings forth a year of action and change.
- A Time for Optimism and Empathy!
- A period of movement and will.
- Unforeseen changes and surprising developments
- A year for transparency, communication, calm, balance and moderation.
- The Water TIGER is synonymous with kindness, alertness, curiosity, intelligence.
- The Water Tiger can be rash, impulsive, dynamic and full of energy.
- The Water TIGER promotes justice, morality and strong leadership.
- 2022 TIGER possess a great sense of morals, is calm, fair and just, confident and self-assured.

Understanding and applying the wonderful science of Feng Shui helps to better adapt to the changing times and energies within our environment, home, country and world . There is always a need to adjust to the dynamic nature of the winds that blow and the waters that flow. Feng Shui literally means "wind and water". Wind is the energy of our breath and water represents how we choose to exist in the flow of life...

May 2022 bring you health harmony and prosperity.

Michele

1

2022 ASTROLOGY AND FENG SHUI

2022 ASTROLOGY AND FENG SHUI

Published by Complete Feng Shui

Mb: 0421 116 799,

Email: michele@completefengshui.com

Websites: www.completefengshui.com

2022 Astrology and Feng Shui ©

Author: Michele Castle

Design copyright @completefengshui

Title: 2022 Astrology and Feng Shui

ISBN: 978-0-6452137-5-1

January 2022

This Planner has been written to offer insight and planning for daily activities and energies of 2022 from Flying Stars, Bagua, Chinese astrology, and date selection. The author editor and publisher take no responsibility for the outcome of any information implemented from this planner.

Platinum member of the Association of Feng Shui Consultants (AFSC)

Recognised Feng Shui training institution by the (AFSC)

facebook@completefengshui   instagram@completefengshui

CONTENTS

COMPLETE FENG SHUI 2022 MONTHLY PLANNER

What is Feng Shui...

Feng Shui means "wind and water." *Wind* **is the energy of our breath.**
Water **represents how we choose to exist in the flow of our life.**

Feng Shui is the ancient art and science of placement, to bring about a balance between people and their environment. It is the study of energy flow through environment and architecture. Feng Shui (pronounced Fung Shway) is a Chinese discipline that seeks to establish harmony and balance in life and the environment. It is an ancient body of knowledge that originated thousands of years ago in China, and it literally means 'wind and water.' Feng Shui is a mathematical, analytical formula-based philosophy taking time dimension into consideration. It reveals how our living space – home, garden office – mirrors our lives. By harnessing the positive aspects of nature, we can create vital new energy.

If we believe the earth is a living thing; everything is alive, everything is interconnected, everything is forever and changing, then Feng Shui affects all.

Traditional Feng Shui combines landforms magnetic influences, eight sectors, Chinese astrology and flying stars.

Today's Feng Shui is similar and practised in many different levels and ways, and with the same goal: to assist in achieving success in all areas of life. Using various methods like landform, eight sector (mansions), Bagua and flying star, all take a systematic approach to addressing problematic areas within a building, home, and environment. Placement, symbolism and tips play a very important role in tricking and manipulating the energy to bring about favourable understanding and outcomes within the home and environment.

We have all experienced Feng Shui in our lives. Many have favorite memories and places; a sense of belonging and security, and harmony within nature and our environment. What you felt was good Feng Shui. The energy of a place, or indeed your own energy, and how the two interact is central to Feng Shui. Feng Shui promises that once you create balance and harmony, you will increase your peace, security, prosperity, happiness, health, love and luck within your living and working environment.

The wonderful thing about Feng Shui is the positive benefit it creates for everyone. Feng Shui is not just about becoming wealthy or achieving success; it is concerned with enriching lives, reducing aggravations, and bringing happiness into relationships. It is about feeling happy, prosperous, and contented. When good Feng Shui energies begin to permeate all areas of life – family, career, health, creativity- you can begin to thrive and prosper

When you know how to be creative in the use of colours, shapes and materials, and know about placement of symbolism and decorative items in your home, you will discover a new energy and zest for life. Life will become joyous; your relationships with loved ones will reach a better level of understanding. Interactions with others will begin to improve.

Feng Shui allows YOU to get to the core issues faster and change the way you live and see life.

HOW DOES FENG SHUI WORK?

Feng Shui and symbolism, the art of placement and the study of energy, can benefit many people. The more you understand, the more you can help yourself. However, just because you have, and practice good Feng Shui does not necessarily mean terrible things will not sometimes happen! However, you will be better protected.

Your Chinese astrology and *Bazi*, or "Four Pillars of Destiny" charts, will determine very much how you perform and are impacted from year to year. Always remember to do the right thing and stay within your values and morals and let karma take care of the rest.

How do you explain Feng Shui in a sentence? If summed up, maybe it would be:

"The Feng Shui system is developed and refined based on elements of astronomy, astrology, geology, mathematics, philosophy, psychology, physics, and divination (intuition)."

Three factors make an impact on your life right now and always. These factors are:

· Heaven Luck.
· Man Luck; and
· Earth Luck

Words of wisdom from a grandmaster:

An old wise man said:
"Heaven luck is the boat given to you by God.
Earth luck is the wind that fills the sails and the currents of the ocean.
Human luck is the way in which you use the wind and the currents to steer your boat."

Meaning:
Heaven luck is your destiny, Earth luck is Feng Shui to smooth the path that brings opportunities, and Human luck is "You" and how you can shape your path, destiny and make use of your opportunities.
These are the components of the cosmic Trinity of Luck.

Your life is always influenced by these three factors. Understanding and mastering the aspects and influences within your environment can have a profound impact on how you are influenced and perform from one year to the next. The Cosmic Trinity is the best way to describe these three factors.

Heaven Luck is the hand you are dealt. It is what is given to you, not by your choosing, but by the energies and forces beyond your control from your date of birth. This is your Bazi or Four Pillars of Destiny chart.
Man, Luck is classified as FREE will and the conscious decisions you make. How you spend your time, which improvements you choose to make to your life. Knowledge, influence, and education empower you to strengthen your man luck and abilities.

HOW DOES FENG SHUI WORK? *(continued)*

Earth Luck is the modern science and our environment, be it the people we hang out with, or the buildings in which we live or work from. These would be classed as Feng Shui influences.

Based on the cosmic trinity, you can blueprint your life and year ahead by paying special attention to your Man Luck, the aspects and influences in your life and environment; Heaven Luck, the element and animal forecast from your Bazi, or Four Pillars of Destiny chart, understand your capabilities, strengths, weaknesses and opportunities; and Earth luck, the Feng Shui or flying stars of your home, environment, and the world around you.

The next element is understanding timing and the significant impact it has on results and aspirations, and finally, of course, is ACTION, or understanding when to act and when to lay low. Simply put, "FATE is when the girl of your dreams walks into the room. DESTINY is if you decide to approach her or not." Your life and choices are always about the actions you take.

The wonderful thing about Feng Shui is the positive benefits it can create for everyone. Feng Shui is not just about becoming wealthy or achieving success – it is concerned with enriching lives, reducing aggravations, and bringing happiness into relationships. It is about feeling happy, prosperous, and contented.

When you know how to orientate your doors, organise the layout of rooms, arrange furniture, be creative in the use of colours, shapes, and materials, and know about the placement of decorative items in your home, you will discover a new energy and zest for life. Life will become joyous and your relationships with loved ones will reach a better level of understanding. Interactions with others living in the home will begin to improve, too!

If you also know how to keep your Feng Shui up to date from one year to the next, the benefits will be even greater. When your home enjoys good Feng Shui, it literally becomes infused with harmonious energy and an atmosphere of general health is greatly improved. Your home, now happy and calm, will become a real haven, a sanctuary - just as a home should be!

Feng Shui is easily applied. The main rule is to keep the Chi (life force energy) moving – never let it stagnate or become unbalanced. Sound, activity, movement, and people all keep Chi in motion. When a space stays too still and is neglected for a period, it stagnates. However, the simple act of moving the furniture and using different areas of your home will shift the energy, making you feel much better.

The arrangement of our home space is something many of us take for granted. Often, we focus our attention purely on the aesthetic aspect of arrangement and décor. Insufficient consideration is given to Feng Shui design implications. Correct Feng Shui inputs can improve the luck of almost every home, irrespective of style or decoration.

At worst, bad Feng Shui and negative elements lead to anger, loss, and even violence. Bad Feng Shui means negatives are present, causing many problems such as health issues and monetary loss. If the cause of bad energy is not addressed, you will continue to suffer challenging times.

HOW DOES FENG SHUI WORK? *(continued)*

TIME AFFLICTIONS

The other aspect of Feng Shui that must be accounted for is time. While *physical afflictions* are the result of placement (design, blockages and orientation), *time afflictions* are caused by the passing of time. Therefore, we have two dimensions that influence Feng Shui: space and time. To ensure that you make the best of *time energy*, you need to update your Feng Shui in accordance with changing time.

The Chinese place great emphasis on the calendar. The main Chinese calendar is the lunar calendar. Each cycle of calendar time is expressed in terms of the Five Elements: Fire, Earth, Metal, Water and Wood. These Five Elements, combined with the twelve animals, make a major cycle that lasts for sixty years.

As we move from one year to the next, energy changes, transforming from Yin to Yang, from element to element and from one animal sign to the next. Depending on the ruling element and animal from one month to the next, the energy in the home and its resident's change. Time exerts a very strong impact on your Feng Shui, luck, and destiny.
Good Feng Shui cannot and does not last forever. It must be recharged with small but significant changes every year. Energy must be refreshed, reorganised, and re-energized; spaces and places need rejuvenating and energy must keep moving.

The Flying Stars formula of Feng Shui is a technical approach that directly addresses the effect of time on the energy of homes and businesses.

You can tell from month to month where illness energy lingers. This can be suppressed with remedies. Most importantly, you can stop monetary loss, broken relationships, frustration, disharmony, and the pernicious effect of aggravating people with the correct application of cures and enhancers.

By investing the time and effort of Feng Shui in your home, you will have added a valuable resource to your life. After enhancing the energy of your surroundings with Feng Shui, your view and approach to living spaces will never be the same again.

FLYING STAR FENG SHUI

Getting your Feng Shui right for the coming year and energising the auspicious sectors of 2022 will help ensure you have a smooth-sailing and successful year ahead.

As we move from one year to the next, energy changes. Transforming from Yin to Yang, from element to element, from one animal sign to the next. Depending on the ruling element and animal, from one month to the next the energy in the home and its occupant's also changes. Time exerts a very strong impact on your Feng Shui, your luck and destiny.

Good Feng Shui cannot and does not last forever. It must be recharged with small, but significant changes every year. Energy must be refreshed, reorganised and re-energised. Spaces and places need rejuvenating. Energy must be kept moving.

The Flying Stars formula of Feng Shui is a technical approach that directly addresses the effect of time on the energy of homes and businesses and holds a wonderful promise which enables you to improve your luck tremendously. The 2022 Feng Shui chart maps out the distribution of energy in each of the eight sectors of the compass, as well as the center.

The best strategy is always to take care of the negative Stars first, and then concentrate on boosting the good Stars. Pay closer attention to the sectors where your main door, living room and bedrooms are located. The luck present in the main door and living room sector affects everyone in the household, while the bedroom alters the luck of those who sleep in it.

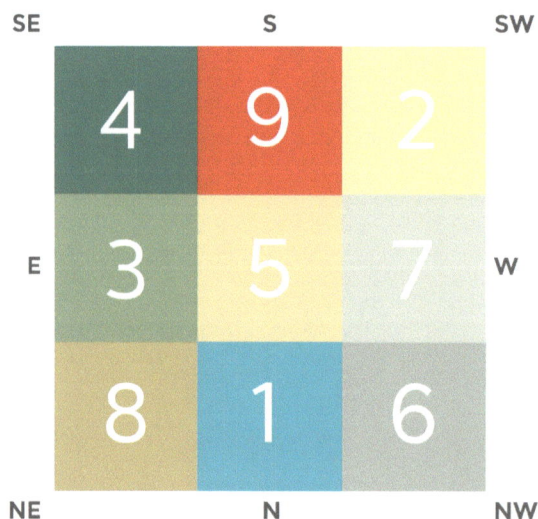

SE	S	SW
4	9	2
E 3	5	7 **W**
8	1	6
NE	N	NW

The daily Flying Star number reveals the energy of the day. By understanding the Flying Stars meaning and energy you can determine the quality of luck for each day.

HOW TO USE THE COMPLETE FENG SHUI PLANNER

Clarity and good timing are vital in ensuring whatever you undertake is given the best possible chance of success. Even simple everyday activities can lead to huge negative outcomes if they are riddled with obstacles and bad energy.

ACTIVITY ICONS

This diary contains specially calculated auspicious dates for significant activities like travelling, moving, renovating, having a haircut or signing a contract. These are marked by icons on each page.

✈ Travelling   🏠 Moving   🏠 Renovating   ✂ Haircut   ✒ Signing Contarct

Understanding The Icons

FAVOURABLE DAYS FOR SPECIFIC TASKS

The icons on each page reveal favourable days for travelling, love and relationship luck, harmonious days, making friends, moving house, signing contracts, having a haircut, starting construction and renovating.

✈ Travelling   ❤ Love and relationship luck   🌸 Harmonious day   🤝 To meeting friends   🏠 Moving

✒ Signing Contarct   ✂ Haircut   🏠 Renovating

Unfavorable days are also indicated for poor health with low life force energy and major activities on clash days.

🔋 Health   ⚡ Major activity's day of clash

Use the waxing cycle of the moon for initiating new projects and the waning cycle for terminating activities.

🌒 🌕 🌘

THE LUNAR CYCLE

Taking note of the lunar cycle enables with choosing the best date for activities. The period between the new and full moon is known as the waxing cycle and is a favourable time for undertaking activities which need growth energy i.e., starting a new project, new journey, opening a new business or signing a deal. The waning cycle (between full moon and new moon) is a good period to shut down something as this is a period when the moon's energy is declining, i.e., closing your business, putting things into storage, finalising a divorce, ending a relationship, starting a diet, quitting smoking, are all good activities during this period.

LOCATION OF THE TAI SUI IN DIFFERENT YEARS

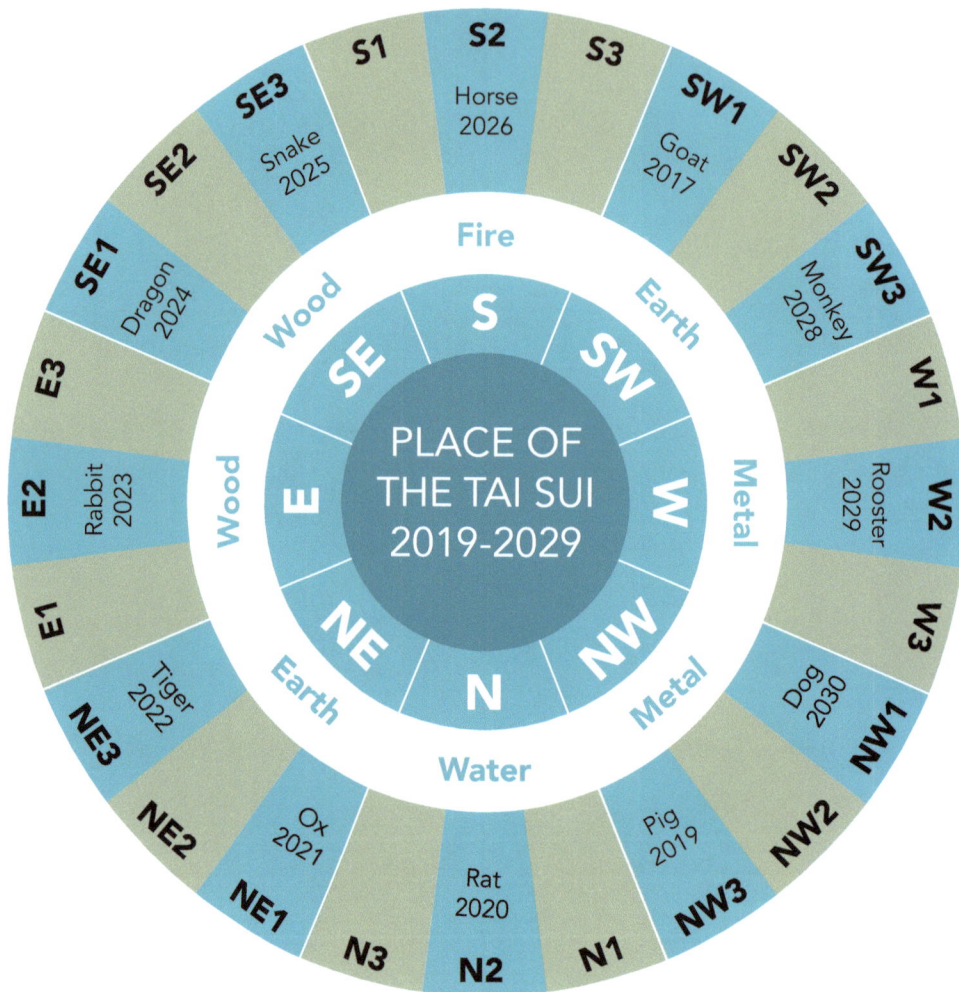

Diagram labels: S1, S2, S3, SW1, SW2, SW3, W1, W2, W3, NW1, NW2, NW3, N1, N2, N3, NE1, NE2, NE3, E1, E2, E3, SE1, SE2, SE3

Snake 2025, Horse 2026, Goat 2017, Monkey 2028, Rooster 2029, Dog 2030, Pig 2019, Rat 2020, Ox 2021, Tiger 2022, Rabbit 2023, Dragon 2024

Fire, Earth, Metal, Metal, Water, Earth, Wood, Wood

Inner ring: SE, S, SW, E, W, NE, N, NW

PLACE OF THE TAI SUI 2019-2029

This year 2022

Each year the Tai Sui follows the changing animal sign and moves his residence to the location of the new animal sign. In the Water Tiger Year of 2022, the Tai Sui moves from the Ox direction (Northeast 1) to the direction and location of the Tiger, which is Northeast 3.

Try not to "offend" the Tai Sui by renovating, banging or digging in his location. You must also avoid facing him while dining, studying, working or closing deals. Doing any of this will bring misfortune. The best method of dealing with the Tai Sui is to appease him with a pair of Pi Yao. You should also place the Tai Sui Plaque 2022 in his location of Northeast 3.

FAVOURABLE STARS

★1 ★4 ★6 ★8 ★9

North 1 Victory Triumph and Success Star (Water Element): Helps attain victory over competition, enhances career promotion and monetary growth. Strengthen and enhance energy by placement of a Victory Horse, Ruyi, or Dragon Tortoise. A water feature would also be especially beneficial.

Southeast 4 Romance and Literacy Star (Wood Element): Good Star which improves relationship opportunities and study and literary fortune for writers and scholars. Enhance luck with bright lights fire energy and wood energy. Place Mandarin Ducks or Huggers, along with peach blossom animals, plants and fresh flowers in this area.

Northwest 6 Heavenly Luck Star (Metal Element): Associated with good fortune and help from heaven, brings speculative luck as well as power and authority. Use bright lights, a water feature and Metal to enhance such as Six Gold Coins on red tassel, and Gold Ingots within this area. A Horse will also assist.

Northeast 8 Current Prosperity Star (Earth Element): Signifies wealth, prosperity, success and happiness; regarded as the most auspicious Star of all the nine numbers until 2024... Strengthen and enhance by placing any form of wealth symbolism such as a Buddha, Wealth God, Six Gold Coins on red tassel, or Gold Ingots, and a water feature or a picture of water in this area. Activate and use the area as often as possible.

South 9 Multiplying Future Prosperity Star (Fire Element): Signifies future prosperity; spurs celebrations, festivities, gatherings and excellent good luck. Enhance the south with bright lights, any wealth symbolism such as a Buddha, a Wealth God, 9 Gold Coins on red tassel, or Gold Ingots.

SE	S	SW
4	9	2
E 3	5	7 **W**
8	1	6
NE	N	NW

UNFAVOURABLE STARS

★ 2 ★ 3 ★ 5 ★ 7

Southwest 2 Sickness Star (Earth Element): This illness bringing Star has negative influences on health issues, bringing physical ailments and diseases. . . Supress the energy with placing a Wu Lou (Health Gourd), Six Gold Coins on red tassel, a Saltwater Cure and a Quan Yin in the South West.

East 3 Hostile, Conflict and Dispute Star (Wood Element): A bad Star which signifies lawsuits, hostility and quarrels. Brings misunderstandings amongst staff, clients and colleagues, and trouble with the authorities. I recommend placing Fire energy in this area such as bright lights, a red piece of paper, or you can use any red décor object. If your front door is in this area I recommend placing Temple Lions and the Evil Eye symbol. Remove any excess water or plants. Remove Metal windchimes. Do not overstimulate with radio or TV energy.

Centre 5 Misfortune and Obstacles Star (Earth Element): Also known as Wu Wang or 5 Yellow Star: It is considered the most malevolent and dangerous of the nine Stars, it brings all kind of misfortunes, accidents, losses and death. Subdue with a Brass 5 element Pagoda, and a Saltwater Cure in the centre. A Ganesha will also assist with removing of obstacles. Keep electrical equipment to a minimum and avoid the colours red and yellow. Try to avoid any major activity within this sector.

West 7 Robbery and Evil Star (Metal Element): This unlucky star brings loss, robbery, violence, and gossip to the West sector. Suppress by placing three pieces of Lucky Bamboo in a vase of water, and bright lights in this area, along with the Evil Eye Symbol, and one Blue Rhinoceros and one Blue Elephant, or two Blue Rhinoceroses for extra protection. If your front door is located here, I also recommend Temple Lions.

ALSO...

In 2022, the **Northeast** (52.6 – 67.5) is also where the Tai Sui "God of the year" (also known as the Grand Duke) will be located for the year. The Grand Duke is an energy point from the universe that is classed as a God which should always be respected and never disturbed or confronted. It is strongly advised that you *avoid any major renovations or any kind of earthmoving* in this sector for the year and keep this area quiet. You can place a Chi Lin, Pi Yao and Fu Dog in the Northeast 3 facing the Southwest 3 - to appease and assist this sector. But best to not disturb in the first place.

In 2022, The Three Killings, which is an energy force, has moved to the **North**. When disturbed, The Three Killings tend to bring sickness and health issues, as well as multiple confrontations. You are best to not sit with The Three Killings behind you, instead you should face them.

It is strongly advised that you avoid any major renovations or any kind of earthmoving in this sector for the year and keep this area quiet. You can place strong plant or earth energy of crystals in the **North** to exhaust Three Killings. But best not to disturb or renovate in the first place.

Compatible Chinese Animals Sign in 2022:	Incompatible Chinese animals in 2022:
Horse, Dog and Pig	Monkey and Snake

Good Travel Directions in 2022:	Lucky colours for 2022:
Southeast, Northwest, North and Northeast	White, Gold, Silver, Blue, and green

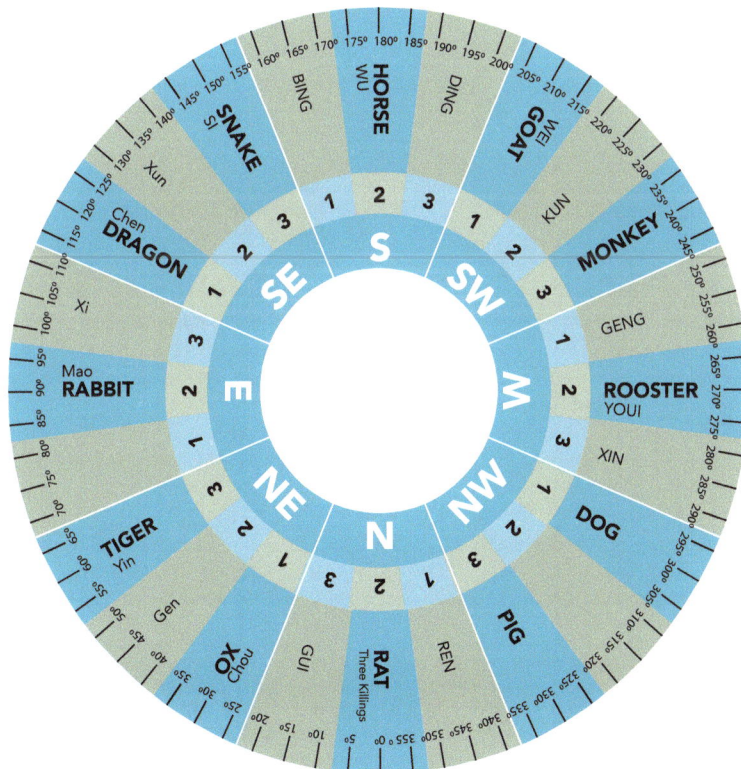

January 2022 Metal Ox (1925, 1937, 1949, 1961, 1973, 1985, 1997, 2009, 2021)

The hardest worker of all the animals; they are persistent, will take the pressure off others, have a high stamina, and will carry heavy burdens. But … they can be stubborn, reveal very little, including their health and will seldom complain. They also tend to stay put for extended periods of time.

Sun	Mon	Tue	Wed	Thur	Fri	Sat
30 water goat	**31** wood monkey *Chinese New Year Jan 31st - Feb 6th*	**GOOD DAYS FOR:** ✈ Travelling ❤ Love and relationship luck 🌺 Harmonious day 👥 Making friends 🏠 Moving house	**GOOD DAYS FOR:** ✒ Signing contracts **BAD DAYS FOR:** 🩹 Health ⚡ Major activity's day of clash			**1** wood tiger *New Year's Day*
2 wood rabbit	**3** fire dragon *New Moon New Year Holiday*	**4** fire snake	**5** earth horse	**6** earth goat	**7** metal monkey	**8** metal rooster
9 water dog	**10** water pig 🌙	**11** wood rat	**12** wood ox	**13** fire tiger	**14** fire rabbit	**15** earth dragon
16 earth snake	**17** metal horse	**18** metal goat 🌕 *Full Moon*	**19** water monkey	**20** water rooster	**21** wood dog	**22** wood pig
23 fire rat	**24** fire ox	**25** earth tiger 🌙	**26** earth rabbit *Australia Day*	**27** metal dragon	**28** metal snake	**29** water horse

For January, the monthly visiting **Flying Star 3** brings **gossip, arguments, legal trouble, conflict, and disputes.**

It is a hostile Star, known for bringing about violence, anger, misunderstandings, constant disagreements, heated arguments, litigation, trouble with authorities and in extreme cases, legal complications between family members, friends and or colleagues.

Health issues related to the liver, gall bladder, feet and arms may arise. As the yearly flying star sits in the Southwest and the Southwest belongs to the earth element. Wood controls the earth so there will also be earth related issues such as digestive problems. Productivity will drop. Relationships between spouses will be affected with high tense energies. Harmony of families and stability of marriages will also be affected. Watch out for trouble with the authorities or you may be hit with litigation. The matriarch, older women, Monkey and Goat born people are the most likely to be affected this month.

Cures to be placed for January include a red piece of paper which is the traditional Chinese cure, or other red and purple décor objects. This includes candles, or bright lights. A magic flaming wheel can be used, or an image of a red phoenix or an eagle. If your front door is in the Southwest sector, you would benefit greatly by placing temple lions there for extra protection along with an evil eye symbol.

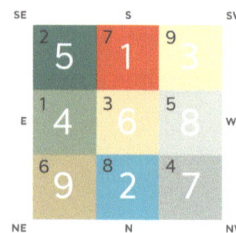

SE	S		SW
5	7 1	9	
E 4	3 6	5 8	W
9	8 2	4 7	
NE	N		NW

Pertaining to the Luo Shu or Bagua school of Feng Shui, the annual flying star 3 sits in the Southwest sector for 2022 this sector is representative of relationship luck, love, romance, and marriage. The Southwest belongs to the element of earth, to enhance the Southwest of your home for positive relationship luck. Use earth and fire energy for support; amethyst, rose quartz crystal, or purple, pink, red peonies. Also, the double happiness symbol, a pair of Mandarin Ducks is symbolism of couples. Additional bright lights are recommended in this sector.

■ Favourable monthly animal - Rat, Snake, Rooster   ■ Unfavourable monthly animal - Goat

February 2022 Water Tiger (1926, 1938, 1950, 1962, 1974, 1986, 1998, 2010, 2022)

Sensitive, alert, has a lot of energy, influential and can be bad tempered. They are usually leaders, take chances and lead fortunate lives. They are also independent and fiercely protective of their family.

Sun	Mon	Tue	Wed	Thur	Fri	Sat
		1 wood rooster *New Moon* — ❤️ 4	**2** fire dog — ⚡ 5	**3** fire pig — 🏠✒️ 6	**4** earth rat — ✈️✒️ 7	**5** earth ox — 🌼 8
6 metal tiger — 🤝 9	**7** metal rabbit — 🤝✈️❤️ 1	**8** water dragon 🌙 — 💧 2	**9** water snake — 3	**10** wood horse — 🤝✈️❤️ 4	**11** wood goat *New Moon* — 🏠⚡ 5	**12** fire monkey — ⚡ 6
13 fire rooster — ✈️ 7	**14** earth dog *Valentine's Day* — 🌼 8	**15** earth pig — ✒️ 9	**16** metal rat — ✈️✒️ 1	**17** metal ox *Full Moon* ☀️ — 💧 2	**18** water tiger — ✒️ 3	**19** water rabbit — ✒️❤️🤝✈️🏠 4
20 wood dragon — 🤝⚡ 5	**21** wood snake — 6	**22** fire horse — 7	**23** fire goat — 🏠🌼 8	**24** earth monkey 🌙 — ⚡ 9	**25** earth rooster — 🏠 1	**26** metal dog — 💧 2
27 metal pig — 🏠 3	**28** water rat — ❤️ 4					

GOOD DAYS FOR:
- ✈️ Travelling
- ❤️ Love and relationship luck
- 🌼 Harmonious day
- 🤝 Making friends
- 🏠 Moving house

GOOD DAYS FOR:
- ✒️ Signing contracts

BAD DAYS FOR:
- 💧 Health
- ⚡ Major activity's day of clash

For February, the monthly visiting **Flying Star 2** brings **turbulent energies, negative people, illness, sickness, disease and stress** to all homes and businesses.

It is an Earth element Star that threatens to bring turbulent energies wreaking havoc on health, illness, disease, and those with existing or persistent health problems. It is believed to worsen an existing illness. In 2022, women, elderly women and pregnant women will be affected by this negative Star the most. In 2022, it will affect you if your front door, main bedroom or living area is in the Southwest; or the Monkey and Goat born person, will experience feeling physically and mentally weak. The flying star 2 has the potential to bring positive property related or real estate investments but it will come at the cost of health.

It is strongly advised to help cure the Southwest of your home and business with a **health gourd**, (also known as a wu lou), six gold coins on red tassel, a saltwater cure, and a Quan yin. If possible, wear a wu lou pendant or carry a wu lou amulet if you are a Monkey or Goat. A metal bell or windchime, can be used but the metal energy is to be reasonably still and heavy, so metal wall sculptures work better.

To counter the effects of this negative star, place heavy metal objects made of brass, cooper, bronze, or pewter in this sector. Metallic artwork, colours, white, silver, gold, and home décor items. Reduce and remove Fire and earth energy.

SE	S	SW
4	9	2
3	5	7
8	1	6

Pertaining to the Luo Shu or Bagua school of Feng Shui, the annual flying star 2 sits in the Southwest sector for 2022 this sector is representative of relationship luck, love, romance, and marriage.

The Southwest belongs to the element of earth, to support aspects of the Southwest of your home for positive relationship luck. Use pink and red peonies, a double happiness symbol, a pair of Mandarin Ducks, and or symbolism of couples in this sector.

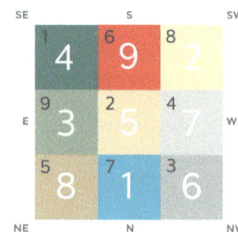

Favourable monthly animal - Pig, Horse and Dog   Unfavourable monthly animal - Monkey

March 2022 Water Rabbit (1915, 1927, 1939, 1951, 1963, 1975, 1987, 1999, 2011, 2023)

Exceptionally sensitive, alert, intelligent and honest. Their minds move at great speeds, they are clever, analytical and will always have back up plans. They are soft, emotional, sensitive and quick tempered, but very rarely express it. They can be impatient, vulnerable and believe it or not, they are a great asset to have.

Sun	Mon	Tue	Wed	Thur	Fri	Sat
		1 water ox `5`	**2** wood tiger `6`	**3** wood rabbit *New Moon* `7`	**4** fire dragon `8`	**5** fire snake `9`
6 earth horse `1`	**7** earth goat `2`	**8** metal monkey `3`	**9** metal rooster `4`	**10** water dog `5`	**11** water pig `6`	**12** wood rat `7`
13 wood ox `8`	**14** fire tiger `9`	**15** fire rabbit `1`	**16** earth dragon `2`	**17** earth snake `3`	**18** metal horse *Full Moon* `4`	**19** metal goat `5`
20 water monkey `6`	**21** water rooster `7`	**22** wood dog `8`	**23** wood pig `9`	**24** fire rat `1`	**25** fire ox `2`	**26** earth tiger `3`
27 earth rabbit `4`	**28** metal dragon `5`	**29** metal snake `6`	**30** water horse `7`	**31** water goat `8`		

GOOD DAYS FOR:
- Travelling
- Love and relationship luck
- Harmonious day
- Making friends
- Moving house

GOOD DAYS FOR:
- Signing contracts

BAD DAYS FOR:
- Health
- Major activity's day of clash

For March, the monthly visiting **Flying Star 1**, known as the **Star of Triumph, fame, wealth, intelligence, and Success**, brings positive energies. This lucky Star is associated with winning attaining success, reputation, good name, status, and fame. It brings excellent triumphant victory over competition, career, and academic pursuits such as writing / research and scholastic success. This lucky star derives remarkable success for wealth opportunities, networking and social circles promoting reputation with influence and victory. This month will effectively enhance noble pursuits, as well as wealth or career related pursuits especially if you are a teen boy Rat born person. Those who enjoy these good influences will be inclined to experience competitive activities.

The Flying Star 1 has a positive influence in attracting victory over past malaise and niggling health concerns. But it is wise to watch out for emotional turbulences such as emotional instability and depression can occur. The Water element brings triumph via Yang energy to this auspicious Star, which you can activate by placing metal objects, like a windchime, or your collection of trophies and medals. A water feature or a Victory Horse figurine and a Ruyi in this sector is also suggested.

SE	S	SW
9 **4**	5 **9**	7 **2**
8 **3**	1 **5**	3 **7**
4 **8**	6 **1**	2 **6**

(E left, W right; NE, N, NW bottom)

Pertaining to the Luo Shu or Bagua school of Feng Shui, the annual flying star 1 sits in the North sector for 2022 this sector is representative of career and business luck. The North belongs to the element of Water. To enhance the North of your home for career and business support and luck, place metal colours like white, silver, gold, pewter, bronze and black to support the water energy, or metal decor objects, with blue black tones or water pictures and décor items. A Black Tortoise or Dragon Tortoise piece can also be used.

Favourable monthly animal - Dog, Goat and Pig   Unfavourable monthly animal - Rooster

7

2

8   3   5   4   9

1

6

HO

TU

April 2022   Wood Dragon (1916, 1928, 1940, 1952, 1964, 1976, 1988, 2000, 2012)

Spirit of great power, wisdom, strength and energy. They can look down on people, but they work and accomplish on grand scale. A love for challenges, in order to gain respect and support of others. They are dreamers, creative, optimistic, steady and firm. Dragons are generally very good in business.

Sun	Mon	Tue	Wed	Thur	Fri	Sat
GOOD DAYS FOR: ✈ Travelling ❤ Love and relationship luck 🌳 Harmonious day 🧡 Making friends 🏠 Moving house	**GOOD DAYS FOR:** ✒ Signing contracts **BAD DAYS FOR:** 📷 Health ⚡ Major activity's day of clash				**1** wood monkey *New Moon* 🏠 ⚡ · 9	**2** wood rooster · 1
3 fire dog ✈ 🏠 📷 · 2	**4** fire pig 🏠 ✒ · 3	**5** earth rat ❤ · 4	**6** earth ox ⚡ · 5	**7** metal tiger ✈ · 6	**8** metal rabbit ❤ · 7	**9** water dragon 🌙 ✈ 🌳 · 8
10 water snake 🏠 · 9	**11** wood horse 🧡 · 1	**12** wood goat 📷 · 2	**13** fire monkey ⚡ · 3	**14** fire rooster ✈ 🏠 ❤ · 4	**15** earth dog *Good Friday* ⚡ · 5	**16** earth pig · 6
17 metal rat *Full Moon* ☀ ✒ · 7	**18** metal ox *Easter Monday* 🌳 · 8	**19** water tiger ✈ 🏠 ✒ · 9	**20** water rabbit ✈ ✒ ❤ · 1	**21** wood dragon ✈ 📷 · 2	**22** wood snake 🏠 · 3	**23** fire horse 🌙 🧡 ✈ ❤ · 4
24 fire goat ⚡ · 5	**25** earth monkey *Anzac Day* ⚡ · 6	**26** earth rooster · 7	**27** metal dog 🌳 · 8	**28** metal pig · 9	**29** water rat · 1	**30** water ox 📷 · 2

For April, the monthly visiting **Flying Star 9** shines brightly. It is the **Star of Future Prosperity, Completion, fame, celebration, wealth intelligence and popularity**, happiness, and recognition. This dynamic and entertaining Fire Star spurs celebrations, festivities, gatherings, and excellent good luck. It is also referred to as the Star of completion because it shows the ability to bring successful fruition to projects started previously. There is notable success in finance and an abundance of luck. It enhances the luck to positive outcomes in the future for the seeds you have previously sown and encourages any endeavour towards boosting your income; especially if you are a teen girl, or Horse born person.

This is also a secondary Star that brings wealth, with boosts to business profits and investments. A raise of fame and recognition. Some believe the Flying Star 9 is more powerful and potent than the Flying Star 8. You are advised to use this space frequently if you wish to start a new business, plan to marry or start a family. Enhance with any wealth symbolism such as wealth jar, Buddha, trinity of horses, 9 Gold Coins on tassel, a Wealth God or Gold Ingots, objects in multiples of nine and keep this part of the home or office brightly lit. Red phoenix, lots of red upholstery and decor here. Nine fish in water an excellent energy enhancer.

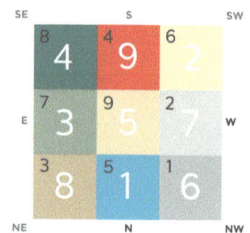

SE	S	SW
8 **4**	4 **9**	6 **2**
7 **3**	9 **5**	2 **7**
3 **8**	5 **1**	1 **6**

(E — left, W — right; NE / N / NW — bottom)

Pertaining to the Luo Shu or Bagua school of Feng Shui, the annual flying star 9 sits in the South sector for 2022, this sector is representative of fame, recognition, and reputation. The South belongs to the element of Fire, to enhance the South of your home for recognition. The South sector is the home of the celestial red phoenix, to triumph over competition with opportunities use the statue of Phoenix or a horse picture or statue to bring speed and endurance in your endeavours. Generally bright lights and objects of red (fire) colours are the most auspicious in the South. Add more wood element such as plants to balance water and fire energy. Galloping Horses or Horse symbolism are the best enhancement.

Favourable monthly animal - Rooster, Rat and Monkey   **Unfavourable monthly animal - Dog**

May 2022 Wood Snake (1917, 1929, 1941, 1953, 1965, 1977, 1989, 2001, 2013)

Has sensitivity, very perceptive, alert and enjoys life to the full. Goal orientated, persistent, alert, loyal, patient, but unforgiving; do not make them your enemy, but they make great friends. Snakes tend to acquire knowledge and then move on. They are determined and can be wise.

Sun	Mon	Tue	Wed	Thur	Fri	Sat
1 wood tiger *New Moon* — 3	**2** wood rabbit — 4	**3** fire dragon — 5	**4** fire snake — 6	**5** earth horse — 7	**6** earth goat — 8	**7** metal monkey — 9
8 metal rooster — 1	**9** water dog — 2	**10** water pig — 3	**11** wood rat — 4	**12** wood ox — 5	**13** fire tiger — 6	**14** fire rabbit — 7
15 earth dragon — 8	**16** earth snake *Full Moon* — 9	**17** metal horse — 1	**18** metal goat — 2	**19** water monkey — 3	**20** water rooster — 4	**21** wood dog — 5
22 wood pig — 6	**23** fire rat — 7	**24** fire ox — 8	**25** earth tiger — 9	**26** earth rabbit — 1	**27** metal dragon — 2	**28** metal snake — 3
29 water horse — 4	**30** water goat *New Moon* — 5	**31** wood monkey — 6				

GOOD DAYS FOR:
- Travelling
- Love and relationship luck
- Harmonious day
- Making friends
- Moving house

GOOD DAYS FOR:
- Signing contracts

BAD DAYS FOR:
- Health
- Major activity's day of clash

For May, the monthly visiting **Flying Star 8** shines bright. It is the **Star of wealth, health, prosperity, fame, finance, and current prosperity** bringing abundant wealth, money, fortune and good luck of wealth, nobility, and steadfastness. You can expect improved income, wealth success and power luck. Professional pursuits, good reputation and efforts acknowledged will flourish if you can tap into this positive month.

If your home has a Northeast main door, living or family area in this sector, everyone in your home will be able to gain from this Star throughout May. Especially if you are a young boy, Ox or Tiger born person.

To allow energy to flow, this area should be kept clutter-free. To activate its luck, any form of wealth symbolism can be placed in this area such as a Buddha, 6 Gold Coins on tassel, a Wealth God or Gold Ingots, as well as bright lights clocks, TV and lots of activity. Remember movement or your footsteps are the most powerful mover of energy.

SE	S	SW
7 4	3 9	5 2
6 3	8 5	1 7
2 8	4 1	9 6
NE	N	NW

Pertaining to the Luo Shu or Bagua School of Feng Shui, the annual flying star 8 sits in the North-East sector for 2022, this sector is representative of knowledge, scholarly, learning and education. The Northeast belongs to the element of Earth, so this is an auspicious location. To support and enhance use a picture of Mountains, a Crystal Globe, world map, Chinese saint Luohan or Dragon Carp. Take note if the North-East sector is blocked by a large tree or missing space, you will have trouble tapping into learning and knowledge.

Favourable monthly animal - Monkey, Ox and Rooster   Unfavourable monthly animal - Pig

June 2022 Fire Horse (1918, 1930, 1942, 1954, 1966, 1978, 1990, 2002. 2014)

Devoted, have inner-strength, persistent, hard workers and determined. They are dependable, honest, and loyal and love challenges. They are proud, independent, but they need companions. Horse's also likes the comforts can be frivolous and love to gossip.

Sun	Mon	Tue	Wed	Thur	Fri	Sat
			1 wood rooster · 7	**2** fire dog · 8	**3** fire pig · 9	**4** earth rat · 1
5 earth ox · 2	**6** metal tiger · 3	**7** metal rabbit · 4	**8** water dragon · 5	**9** water snake · 6	**10** wood horse · 7	**11** wood goat · 8
12 fire monkey · 9	**13** fire rooster · 1	**14** earth dog *Full Moon* · 2	**15** earth pig · 3	**16** metal rat · 4	**17** metal ox · 5	**18** water tiger · 6
19 water rabbit · 7	**20** wood dragon · 8	**21** wood snake · 9/1	**22** fire horse · 9	**23** fire goat · 8	**24** earth monkey · 7	**25** earth rooster · 6
26 metal dog · 5	**27** metal pig · 4	**28** water rat · 3	**29** water ox *New Moon* · 2	**30** wood tiger · 1		

GOOD DAYS FOR:
- Travelling
- Love and relationship luck
- Harmonious day
- Making friends
- Moving house

GOOD DAYS FOR:
- Signing contracts

BAD DAYS FOR:
- Health
- Major activity's day of clash

For June, the monthly visiting inauspicious **Flying Star 7**, brings conflict, arguments, lawsuits, illness, accidents, **Robbery and Gossip**. The Flying Star 7 is much feared because of this potential of rivalry, theft, burglary, loss of wealth and violence that it can bring into one's life. It is important to be cautious during this month. It will mainly have an adverse effect on emotional and physical wellbeing especially if you are a young girls or Rooster born person. Office politics and competitions will be high. Being swindled by others is a real possibility. Watch your back during this month and be careful who you trust. Scams and trickeries are just around the corner. Be cautious if principal areas are open and in the West. Strong emotions, robbery, gossips, and villains can be averted if you steer clear of the West area.

Sickness related to the mouth and teeth may surface. There is the possibility of hospitalisation or surgery for those with existing health complications. Remedy this Star with the traditional cure of three pieces of Bamboo in a transparent glass vase of water in the Western location; the Evil Eye symbol with seven glass elephants, or place one Blue Rhinoceros and one Blue Elephant, or a pair of Blue Rhinoceros figurines in this sector, facing out of the home. A water feature also helps exhausting the metal energy of the flying star 7.

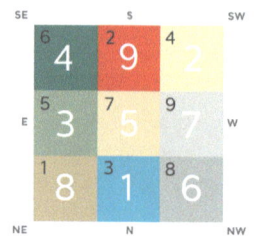

SE	S	SW
6 · **4**	2 · **9**	4 · **2**
5 · **3** (E)	7 · **5**	9 · **7** (W)
1 · **8** (NE)	3 · **1** (N)	8 · **6** (NW)

Pertaining to the Luo Shu or Bagua school of Feng Shui, the annual flying star 7 sits in the West sector for 2022, this sector is representative of descendants, family and children luck, and the protection of your current assets and wealth.
The West sector is the home of the celestial white tiger, so placing the symbolism of Tiger in the West can protect the luck of the family. Place any wealth symbolism in the West area to assist protection and for the family to stay together remaining healthy and strong. The West belongs to the element of Metal. For 2022 enhance wealth luck with Gold Coins, Gold Ingots, a Wealth God, metallic artwork, paintings or colours. The West wall is the favorable position for family photos in metallic frames.

☐ **Favourable monthly animal - Goat, Tiger and Pig**   ☐ **Unfavourable monthly animal - Rat**

July 2022 Fire Goat (1919, 1931, 1943, 1955, 1967, 1979, 1991, 2003, 2015)

Stable, determined, hardworking, and willing. They are survivors, not a leader, but make effective team worker. They are observant, great listeners and need to have people around them. Goats like harmony but do not like to be alone.

Sun	Mon	Tue	Wed	Thur	Fri	Sat
31 wood rooster _[6]_	**GOOD DAYS FOR:** 🛫 Travelling · ❤️ Love and relationship luck · 🌳 Harmonious day · Making friends · 🏠 Moving house	**GOOD DAYS FOR:** 🖊️ Signing contracts · **BAD DAYS FOR:** Health · ⚡ Major activity's day of clash			**1** wood rabbit ❤️ _[9]_	**2** fire dragon 🌱 _[8]_
3 fire snake _[7]_	**4** earth horse ⚡ _[6]_	**5** earth goat ⚡ 🛫🏠🖊️ _[5]_	**6** metal monkey ⚡ 🛫🏠❤️ _[4]_	**7** metal rooster 🌙 🛫🖊️ _[3]_	**8** water dog 🩹 _[2]_	**9** water pig _[1]_
10 wood rat _[9]_	**11** wood ox 🌳 _[8]_	**12** fire tiger 🛫🏠 _[7]_	**13** fire rabbit 🛫🏠❤️ _[6]_	**14** earth dragon _Full Moon_ 🌕 ⚡ _[5]_	**15** earth snake 🏠🖊️❤️ _[4]_	**16** metal horse _[3]_
17 metal goat 🛫🏠🩹 _[2]_	**18** water monkey ⚡ _[1]_	**19** water rooster 🛫 _[9]_	**20** wood dog 🌙 🌱 _[8]_	**21** wood pig 🏠 _[7]_	**22** fire rat _[6]_	**23** fire ox ⚡ _[5]_
24 earth tiger ❤️ 🛫🏠🖊️ _[4]_	**25** earth rabbit ❤️ 🛫🏠🖊️ _[3]_	**26** metal dragon 🩹 _[2]_	**27** metal snake _[1]_	**28** water horse 🛫🌱 _[9]_	**29** water goat _New Moon_ 🖊️⚡ _[8]_	**30** wood mokey ⚡ _[7]_

For July, there will be the monthly visiting **Flying Star 6**, a **Star bringing authority, power, wealth, speculative, windfall heaven luck** that is poised to bring good fortune, encouraging manifestation of career prospects. It is said to bring enhanced power, status, authority, good name, and prosperity luck as well as career luck straight from heaven. It is also known as an indirect wealth Star of good luck also straight from heaven that bodes well for professional activities, especially if you want to climb the career ladder or achieve higher recognition at work. The Patriarch, older men, Dog and Pig are the most likely to benefit. The authority that is brought upon by the positive aspects of this Star can also indicate status and influence in social circles.

Bring life to this Star with Yang energy such as water feature, sound, and activity. Traditional enhancers include a Horse figurine, Six Gold Coins on tassel, or Gold Ingots.

If activated by negative external forms the lucky 6 can turn abruptly and bring with its sudden upheavals, changes and medical complications to the kidney or legs.

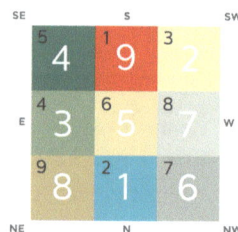

SE	S	SW
5 **4**	1 **9**	3 **2**
4 **3**	5 **5**	7 **7**
9 **8**	2 **1**	7 **6**

(E left, W right; NE bottom-left, N bottom-centre, NW bottom-right)

Pertaining to the Luo Shu or Bagua school of Feng Shui, the annual flying star 6 sits in the North-West sector for 2022, this sector is representative of the man of the house, signifies influential benefactors, mentors, and helpful people. The North West belongs to the element of Metal, in Chinese culture metal also signifies gold. So, this is also a pocket of family wealth. To tap into and enhance, use metal décor items, coloured objects, bells or windchimes. The three Star Gods, represent health, wealth and longevity and are excellent used in the main living area of a home to benefit all occupants

Favourable monthly animal - Horse, Rabbit and Pig   Unfavourable monthly animal - Ox

August 2022 Earth Monkey (1920, 1932, 1944, 1956, 1968, 1980, 1992, 2004, 2016)

Fast thinkers, very quick learners, creative, but can be insensitive. They don't bear grudges, are highly independent and make friends quickly. They are helpful, self-confident, high achievers, ambitious, competitive, and determined and very rarely give up.

Sun	Mon	Tue	Wed	Thur	Fri	Sat
	1 fire dog — 5	**2** fire pig ❤ 4	**3** earth rat 3	**4** earth ox 2	**5** metal tiger 🌙 ✈ ✒ 1	**6** metal rabbit ❤ ✈ 🏠 ✒ 9
7 water dragon 🌿 8	**8** water snake 🏠 ✒ 7	**9** wood horse ✈ ✒ 6	**10** wood goat 🏠 ⚡ 5	**11** fire monkey ✈ ⚡ ❤ 4	**12** fire rooster *Full Moon* ◯ 3	**13** earth dog 🤝 ✈ 🏠 2
14 earth pig 1	**15** metal rat 🏠 9	**16** metal ox 🌿 8	**17** water tiger 7	**18** water rabbit ✈ 🏠 ❤ 6	**19** wood dragon 🌙 🏠 ⚡ 5	**20** wood snake ❤ 4
21 fire horse ✈ 3	**22** fire goat ✈ 🏠 📦 2	**23** earth monkey ✈ ⚡ 1	**24** earth rooster 9	**25** metal dog 🌿 8	**26** metal pig ✈ 7	**27** water rat *New Moon* 6
28 water ox ⚡ 5	**29** wood tiger 4	**30** wood rabbit ❤ 3	**31** fire dragon 🏠 📦 2			

GOOD DAYS FOR:
- ✈ Travelling
- ❤ Love and relationship luck
- 🌿 Harmonious day
- 🤝 Making friends
- 🏠 Moving house

GOOD DAYS FOR:
- ✒ Signing contracts

BAD DAYS FOR:
- 📦 Health
- ⚡ Major activity's day of clash

For August, there will be the monthly visiting **Flying Star 5** (also known as the 5 Yellow Star), the most dangerous, vicious, and aggressive of all Stars. It is the Star of **Danger, misfortune, money loss, problems, bad luck, obstacles, calamities, accidents, illness, and mishaps**. It is always very bad news. It is a malicious Star feared by all Feng Shui-wise as it has the tendency to attract unfavorable outcomes, bad luck of all kinds. This can range from loss of money or salary, that can be very serious. It has been thought to cause major disruption in business plans or even major accidents with serious injuries, which includes fatal accidents. With many damaging manifestations like bankruptcy, betrayals, disloyalty, obstacles, tragedies, mishaps, and anything else that is negative, depressing, and hazardous.

Best not to break ground or attempt new renovation projects. The most effective way to combat the 5 Star is to leave it alone to the best of your ability – do not disturb it! If that is not possible it can be pacified with a Brass Pagoda, Bonze bell, metal windchimes, along with a Saltwater Cure. You can also use a Ganesha to assist with removing of obstacles.

To counter effects of this negative star, you can place heavy Metal objects made of brass, cooper, bronze, or pewter in the Centre of your home. Metallic artwork, colours and home décor items. Reduce and remove Fire and earth energy.

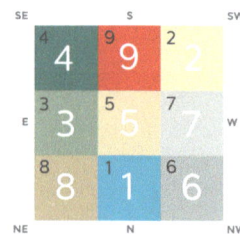

SE	S	SW
4	9	2
3	5	7
8	1	6

Pertaining to the Luo Shu or Bagua school of Feng Shui, the annual flying star 5 sits in the Centre sector for 2022, this sector is representative of health, physical, emotional, and spiritual wellbeing. The Centre belongs to the element of Earth. Earth generates Metal so this is a good relationship. Earth provides foundation and nourishment. The Centre of your home should be open and clear. This allows energy to flow freely and connect all areas to one another. If the energy is blocked in the Centre such as with a staircase or bathroom try to create as much grounded energy as you can with the Earth Element by using square shapes, earthy colours such as yellow and tan, or objects made from earth e.g., ceramic tiles.

Favourable monthly animal - Snake, Rat and Dragon   Unfavourable monthly animal - Tiger

September 2022 Earth Rooster (1921, 1933, 1945, 1957, 1969, 1981, 1993, 2005, 2017)

Unique energy in relationships and friendships. They are musical, creative, artistic, imaginative and inventive; can be drama queens or kings. They can be focused and persistent; know what they want, great talkers, debaters and negotiators. straight forward, honest with others; they make great friends. They are sensitive to relationships, vulnerable and they tend to bottle up their feelings. They will rarely fight back, but when they do it is with full power.

Sun	Mon	Tue	Wed	Thur	Fri	Sat
	GOOD DAYS FOR: Travelling / Love and relationship luck / Harmonious day / Making friends / Moving house	**GOOD DAYS FOR:** Signing contracts **BAD DAYS FOR:** Health / Major activity's day of clash		**1** fire snake — 3	**2** earth horse — 9	**3** earth goat — 8
4 metal monkey (moon) — 7	**5** metal rooster — 6	**6** water dog — 5	**7** water pig — 4	**8** wood rat — 3	**9** wood ox — 2	**10** fire tiger *Full Moon* — 1
11 fire rabbit — 9	**12** earth dragon — 8	**13** earth snake — 7	**14** metal horse — 6	**15** metal goat — 5	**16** water monkey — 4	**17** water rooster — 3
18 wood dog (moon) — 2	**19** wood pig — 1	**20** fire cat — 9	**21** fire ox — 8	**22** earth tiger — 7	**23** earth rabbit — 6	**24** metal dragon — 5
25 metal snake — 4	**26** water horse *New Moon* — 3	**27** water goat — 2	**28** wood monkey — 1	**29** wood rooster — 9	**30** fire dog — 8	

For September, the monthly visiting **Flying Star 4** brings **romance intelligence, talent, wisdom, fame, promotion, academic, scholastic and literacy luck** to all. It is also often called the Peach Blossom Star or a Star of beauty, knowledge, and learning. In 2022, it stands to affect mostly those born in the year of the Dragon and Snake, as well eldest daughters. Generally, this Star brings about harmony and happiness in love relationships. It is highly auspicious for singles that are searching for love and marriage. Bringing about meaningful and fulfilling relationships. Those with a literary, artistic, or creative background such as lecturers, teachers, artists, writers, and researchers will see positive results in their work, with indication of further advancement. Students this month will have better examination luck and better luck in applications for admission to good schools or Universities.

To maintain and enhance love and romance in relationships, couples should strongly consider placing two Rose Quartz crystals next to or under their bed. You can also display love symbols such as Mandarin Ducks, Wish fulfilling birds or Huggers. To enhance Academic luck, display Chinese ink brush / artwork, tiered pagoda, the Chinese saint Luohan or three Star Gods.

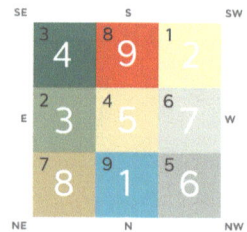

SE	S	SW
3 — **4**	8 — **9**	1 — **2**
2 — **3** (E)	4 — **5**	6 — **7** (W)
7 — **8** (NE)	9 — **1** (N)	5 — **6** (NW)

Pertaining to the Luo Shu or Bagua school of Feng Shui, the annual flying star 4 sits in the South-East sector for 2022, this sector is representative and governed by wealth and prosperity, income, cashflow and earnings. The Southeast belongs to the element of Wood, to tap into money luck enhance this area with a water picture or water feature, water strengthens the wood energy, flowers, plants, green colours and water tones will also help strength the luck. Always make sure the water flow is entering the home and not leaving ...

Favourable monthly animal - Dragon, Ox and Snake   Unfavourable monthly animal - Rabbit

October 2022 Metal Dog (1922, 1934, 1946, 1958, 1970, 1982, 1994, 2006, 2018)

Ready for action, energetic, gains respect, brave but they take risks. They are helpful, loyal, reliable, determined, competent and confident. Dogs will not let go of ideas and ambitions and are likely to see things to the end. They are caring and a great listener. They are very efficient and make great workers, but they are not leaders.

Sun	Mon	Tue	Wed	Thur	Fri	Sat
30 fire dragon [5]	**31** fire snake [4]					**1** fire pig [7]
2 earth rat [6]	**3** earth ox [5]	**4** metal tiger [4]	**5** metal rabbit *New Moon* [3]	**6** water dragon [2]	**7** water snake [1]	**8** wood horse [9]
9 wood goat [8]	**10** fire monkey *Full Moon* [7]	**11** fire rooster [6]	**12** earth dog [5]	**13** earth pig [4]	**14** metal rat [3]	**15** metal ox [2]
16 water tiger [1]	**17** water rabbit [9]	**18** wood dragon [8]	**19** wood snake [7]	**20** fire horse [6]	**21** fire goat [5]	**22** earth monkey [4]
23 earth rooster [3]	**24** metal dog [2]	**25** metal pig *New Moon* [1]	**26** water rat [9]	**27** water ox [8]	**28** wood tiger [7]	**29** wood rabbit [6]

For October, the monthly visiting **Flying Star 3** brings **gossip, arguments, legal trouble, conflict, and disputes**. It is a hostile Star, known for bringing about violence, anger, misunderstandings, constant disagreements, heated arguments, litigation, trouble with authorities and in extreme cases, legal complications between family members, friends and or colleagues.

Health issues related to the liver, gall bladder, feet and arms may arise. As the yearly flying star sits in the East and the East belongs to the wood element. Relationships between spouses will be affected with high tension energies. Harmony of families and stability of marriages will be affected. Watch out for trouble with the authorities or you may be hit with litigation. Eldest sons, and Rabbits are the most likely to be affected.

Cures to be placed for October include a red piece of paper which is the traditional Chinese cure, or other red and purple décor objects, candles, or bright lights. A Magic Flaming Wheel can also be used. The red phoenix or the image of an eagle. If your front door is in the East sector, it would benefit you greatly by placing Temple Lions there for extra protection along with an Evil Eye Symbol.

SE	S	SW
2 **4**	7 **9**	9 **2**
1 **3**	3 **5**	5 **7**
6 **8**	8 **1**	4 **6**

Pertaining to the Luo Shu or Bagua school of Feng Shui, the annual flying star 3 sits in the East sector for 2022, this sector is representative of good health and longevity. The East belongs to the element of Wood, enhance for positive health and wellbeing by strengthen with water and wood therefore lucky bamboo in water is such a powerful cure. Greenery, plants, and flowers are also acceptable to strengthen the sector. The east sector is the home of the celestial green dragon, so placing the symbolism of dragon in the East can maximise the luck of the family. A Quan Yin can also be used to safeguard health and wellbeing.

Favourable monthly animal - Rabbit, Tiger and Horse   Unfavourable monthly animal - Dragon

November 2022 Metal Pig (1923, 1935, 1947, 1959, 1971, 1983 1995, 2007, 2019)

Energy of Wealth in many forms has a sense of time, not in a hurry, can be sluggish and not ambitious. Not very intellectually competitive and has natural humility. They accumulate and are usually rotund. They are accepting, intelligent, perceptive, and independent and can be considerably determined. They are also reliable and wise in times of a crisis.

Sun	Mon	Tue	Wed	Thur	Fri	Sat
		1 earth horse 🌙 ✈️ 🏠 3	**2** earth goat 📦 2	**3** metal monkey ⚡ ✈️ 🏠 🖊️ 1	**4** metal rooster *New Moon* 9	**5** water dog ✈️ 🏠 🎋 8
6 water pig ✈️ 7	**7** wood rat 🤝 ✈️ 6	**8** wood ox ☀️ *Full Moon* 🤝 ⚡ 5	**9** fire tiger 🖊️ ❤️ 🤝 ✈️ 🏠 4	**10** fire rabbit 🤝 🏠 ❤️ 3	**11** earth dragon 📦 2	**12** earth snake 1
13 metal horse ✈️ 🏠 9	**14** metal goat 🤝 🖊️ 🎋 8	**15** water monkey ⚡ 7	**16** water rooster 🌙 6	**17** water dog ✈️ ⚡ 5	**18** wood pig ✈️ ❤️ 4	**19** fire rat 3
20 fire ox 📦 2	**21** earth tiger ✈️ 🏠 🖊️ 1	**22** earth rabbit ✈️ 🏠 ❤️ 9	**23** metal dragon 🎋 8	**24** metal snake *New Moon* 7	**25** water horse ✈️ 🏠 🖊️ 6	**26** water goat 🤝 ⚡ 5
27 wood monkey ⚡ ❤️ 4	**28** wood rooster 3	**29** fire dog 📦 2	**30** fire pig 🌙 1			

GOOD DAYS FOR:
- ✈️ Travelling
- ❤️ Love and relationship luck
- 🎋 Harmonious day
- 🤝 Making friends
- 🏠 Moving house

GOOD DAYS FOR:
- 🖊️ Signing contracts

BAD DAYS FOR:
- 📦 Health
- ⚡ Major activity's day of clash

For November, the monthly visiting **Flying Star 2** brings **turbulent energies, negative people, illness, sickness, disease and stress** to all homes and businesses.

It is an Earth element Star that threatens to bring turbulent energies wreaking havoc on health, illness, disease, and those with existing or persistent health problems. It is believed to worsen an existing illness. In 2022, the matriarch, elderly and pregnant women will be affected by this negative Star the most. In 2022, it will affect you if your front door is in the Southwest, main bedroom or living area; or Monkey and Goat born people, will experience feeling physically and mentally weak. The flying star 2 has the potential to bring positive property related or real estate investments but it will come at the cost of health.

It is strongly advised to help cure the Southwest of your home and business with a Health Gourd, (also known as a Wu Lou), Six Gold Coins on red tassel, a Saltwater Cure, and a Quan Yin. If possible, wear a Wu Lou pendant or carry a Wu Lou amulet if you are a Monkey or a Goat. Metal bell or windchime, can be used but the Metal energy is to be reasonably still and heavy, so metal wall sculptures work better instead.

To counter effects of this negative star, you can place heavy Metal objects made of brass, cooper, bronze, or pewter in this sector. Metallic artwork, colours, white, silver, gold, and home décor items. Reduce and remove Fire and earth energy.

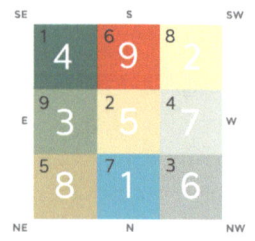

SE	S	SW
4	9	2
3	5	7
8	1	6

(E on left, W on right; NE bottom-left, N bottom-middle, NW bottom-right)

Pertaining to the Luo Shu or Bagua school of Feng Shui, the annual flying star 1 sits in the Southwest sector for 2022 this sector is representative of relationship luck, love, romance, and marriage. The Southwest belongs to the element of earth, to enhance the Southwest of your home for positive relationship luck, use earth and fire energy to support, amethyst, rose quartz crystal, purple, pink, red peonies, double happiness symbol, a pair of Mandarin Ducks, symbolism of couples and bright lights is recommended in this sector.

Favourable monthly animal - Tiger, Rabbit and Goat   **Unfavourable monthly animal - Snake**

December 2022　Water Rat (1924, 1936, 1948, 1960, 1972, 1984, 1996, 2008, 2020)

Enduring, persistent, adaptable, accepting, brave, curious and forgiving. Can talk too freely and can be accused of gossiping. They are fast, determined, they don't stay put and have many changes and moves in all areas of their lives; they are excited by new things.

Sun	Mon	Tue	Wed	Thur	Fri	Sat
	GOOD DAYS FOR: 🛩 Travelling ❤️ Love and relationship luck 🎋 Harmonious day 🎆 Making friends 🏠 Moving house	**GOOD DAYS FOR:** 🖊 Signing contracts **BAD DAYS FOR:** 🩺 Health ⚡ Major activity's day of clash		**1** earth rat — 🛩 🏠 · 9	**2** earth ox — 🤝 🎋 · 8	**3** metal tiger — 🛩 🏠 🖊 · 7
4 metal rabbit — ❤️ 🛩 🏠 🖊 · 6	**5** water dragon — ⚡ · 5	**6** water snake — ❤️ · 4	**7** wood horse — · 3	**8** wood goat *Full Moon* 🟡 — 🛩 🏠 🩺 · 2	**9** fire monkey — 🛩 🏠 ⚡ · 1	**10** fire rooster — · 9
11 earth dog — 🎆 · 8	**12** earth pig — 🛩 · 7	**13** metal rat — · 6	**14** metal ox — 🛩 ⚡ · 5	**15** water tiger — 🖊 ❤️ · 4	**16** water rabbit 🌙 — ❤️ · 3	**17** wood dragon — 🩺 · 2
18 wood snake — 🏠 · 1	**19** fire horse — · 9	**20** fire goat — 🎋 · 8	**21** earth monkey — ⚡ · 7	**22** earth rooster — ❤️ · 6/4	**23** metal dog *New Moon* — ⚡ · 5	**24** metal pig *Christmas Eve* — · 6
25 water rat *Christmas Day* — · 7	**26** water ox *Boxing Day* 🎋 — 🛩 🏠 🖊 · 8	**27** wood tiger — 🖊 · 9	**28** wood rabbit — ❤️ · 1	**29** fire dragon — 🩺 · 2	**30** fire snake 🌙 — · 3	**31** earth horse *New Year's Eve* — ❤️ · 4

For December, the monthly visiting **Flying Star 1**, known as the **Star of Triumph, fame, wealth, intelligence, and Success**, brings positive energies. This lucky Star is associated with winning attaining success, reputation, good name, status, and fame. It brings excellent triumphant, victory over competition, career, and academic pursuits such as writing / research and scholastic success. This lucky star derives remarkable success for wealth opportunities, networking and social circles promoting reputation with influence and victory. This month will effectively enhance noble pursuits, as well as wealth or career related pursuits especially if you are a middle son or Rat born person. Those who enjoy these good influences will be inclined to experience competitive activities.

The Flying Star 1 has a positive influence in attracting victory over past malaise and niggling health concerns. But it is wise to watch out for emotional turbulences such as emotional instability and depression can occur. The Water element brings triumph via Yang energy to this auspicious Star, which you can activate by placing metal objects, windchime your collection of trophies and medals. water feature, a Victory Horse figurine and a Ruyi in this sector.

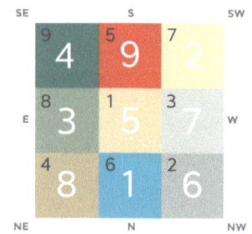

SE	S	SW
4	9	7
3	5	7
8	1	6

(E row: 8 1 3 ; NE 4 8 6 ; N 1 ; NW 6)

Pertaining to the Luo Shu or Bagua school of Feng Shui, the annual flying star 1 sits in the North sector for 2022 this sector is representative of career and business luck. The North belongs to the element of Water, to enhance the North of your home for career and business support and luck place metal colours like white, silver, gold, pewter, bronze and black to support the water energy, metal decor objects, blue black tones or water pictures and décor items. A Black Tortoise or Dragon Tortoise.

Favourable monthly animal - Ox, Monkey and Dragon　　**Unfavourable monthly animal - Horse**

2023 CALENDAR

January

Mo	Tu	We	Th	Fr	Sa	Su
						1
2	3	4	5	6	7	8
9	10	11	12	13	14	15
16	17	18	19	20	21	22
23	24	25	26	27	28	29
30	31					

February

Mo	Tu	We	Th	Fr	Sa	Su
		1	2	3	4	5
6	7	8	9	10	11	12
13	14	15	16	17	18	19
20	21	22	23	24	25	26
27	28					

March

Mo	Tu	We	Th	Fr	Sa	Su
		1	2	3	4	5
6	7	8	9	10	11	12
13	14	15	16	17	18	19
20	21	22	23	24	25	26
27	28	29	30	31		

April

Mo	Tu	We	Th	Fr	Sa	Su
					1	2
3	4	5	6	7	8	9
10	11	12	13	14	15	16
17	18	19	20	21	22	23
24	25	26	27	28	29	30

May

Mo	Tu	We	Th	Fr	Sa	Su
1	2	3	4	5	6	7
8	9	10	11	12	13	14
15	16	17	18	19	20	21
22	23	24	25	26	27	28
29	30	31				

June

Mo	Tu	We	Th	Fr	Sa	Su
			1	2	3	4
5	6	7	8	9	10	11
12	13	14	15	16	17	18
19	20	21	22	23	24	25
26	27	28	29	30		

2023 CALENDAR

July

Mo	Tu	We	Th	Fr	Sa	Su
					1	2
3	4	5	6	7	8	9
10	11	12	13	14	15	16
17	18	19	20	21	22	23
24	25	26	27	28	29	30
31						

August

Mo	Tu	We	Th	Fr	Sa	Su
	1	2	3	4	5	6
7	8	9	10	11	12	13
14	15	16	17	18	19	20
21	22	23	24	25	26	27
28	29	30	31			

September

Mo	Tu	We	Th	Fr	Sa	Su
				1	2	3
4	5	6	7	8	9	10
11	12	13	14	15	16	17
18	19	20	21	22	23	24
25	26	27	28	29	30	

October

Mo	Tu	We	Th	Fr	Sa	Su
						1
2	3	4	5	6	7	8
9	10	11	12	13	14	15
16	17	18	19	20	21	22
23	24	25	26	27	28	29
30	31					

November

Mo	Tu	We	Th	Fr	Sa	Su
		1	2	3	4	5
6	7	8	9	10	11	12
13	14	15	16	17	18	19
20	21	22	23	24	25	26
27	28	29	30			

December

Mo	Tu	We	Th	Fr	Sa	Su
				1	2	3
4	5	6	7	8	9	10
11	12	13	14	15	16	17
18	19	20	21	22	23	24
25	26	27	28	29	30	31

THE FOUR CELESTIAL GUARDIANS

Dressing tables should not face the bed directly. The mirror will cause bad luck and friction in relationships.

Traditional blues and greys bring a very calm coastal feel to a home's energy... be mindful when decorating in this style that the space does not become and feel too cold or emotions will be strong... strengthen and balance with plants and pop of fire by implimenting candles and bright lights...

Display Goldfish for luck. An excellent way to activated energy inside the home is with 9 goldfish in an aquarium or art system.

Warm up the bedroom, add a splash of blush, pink, purple, maroon, plum or red... the bedroom needs to be inviting and represents what you want out of your relationship... red adds passion...

The most auspicious location for your home is determined by the position of the four celestial guardians, which form an armchair configuration.

The Black Turtle is represented by mountains or hills behind the home.

These hills should be higher to act as support and protection for the residents.

The Green Dragon is represented by rolling hills to the left of the home. These hills should be higher than hills to the right of the home.

The White Tiger is represented by hills to the right of the home. Hills to the right should be lower than the left.

The Crimson Phoenix should be a hillock and found in fron of the home. This represents a footstool.

If the configuration of your land is not ideal, you can improve your feng shui by placing images of the four celestial guardians to symbolise their presence in the home.

BEGINNERS FENG SHUI 'EASY TIPS TO ENHANCE EVERYDAY LIVING'

A beginner's guide to learning the fundamentals of Feng Shui and energy flow in the home, known as Chi. This ancient art of placement which brings balance, helps to improve the harmony and prosperity within your space. Ideal as a gift for the novice wanting to learn more or beautiful coffee table book to inspire you on your next home renovation.

Buy Beginners Feng Shui **www.completefengshui.com**

Ebook Beginners Feng Shui **www.completefengshui.com**

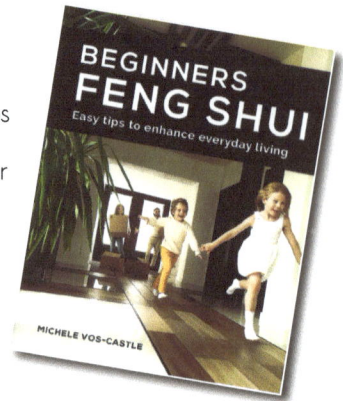

COMPLETE FENG SHUI NEWS IS FOR YOU - TO NAVIGATE AND UNDERSTAND YOURSELF AND ENVIRONMENT: Monthly Subscription

- Monthly Feng Shui and Flying Star Outlook
- All 12 Animals Chinese Horoscope Forecasts and Day Masters
- Calendar Auspicious date selection... And much, much more
- Over 40 pages to navigate monthly Feng Shui

Subscribe **www.completefengshui.com**

COURSES / WORKSHOPS

2022 Year of Water Tiger Astrology & Feng Shui

2022 Complete Lifestyle Retreat

Understanding Feng Shui and your home

Landform and Symbolism... making the most of your home and interior

Show Me the Money – Chinese Astrology for Career, Wealth and Success

Lifestyle Feng Shui – Better Living with Feng Shui – Learn Compass School

Good Feng Shui... property and Real Estate

Getting to Know YOU, Beginners Chinese Astrology Part 1 & 2

Module 1 : Health, Wealth & Prosperity

Module 2: Four Pillars of Destiny Part 1 & 2

Module 3: Flying Stars Part 1 & 2

Module 4:Practitioners Course and Business Practices for a Feng Shui Business

Feng Shui Refresher workshop

Feng Shui as a Business and Career

www.completefengshui.com

info@completefengshui.com.au

MB 0421 116 799

What's App 0421 116 799

Activating Feng Shui in the Garden

Each direction has an element. Use the productive cycle to enhance the element.
Use colours to symbolically create the presence of these elements.

SOUTHEAST

The element of
SMALL WOOD
is associated with
the colour light GREEN,
young growing plants,
anything rectangular, the
season of spring and
expanding energy.

SOUTH

The element of FIRE
is associated with
the colour RED,
bright sunlight, the
glow of lamps, anything
sharp or pointed, the
season of summer and
upwards rising energy.

SOUTHWEST

The element of BIG
EARTH is associated with
the colour OCHRE, stones
and pebbles, boulders
and crystals, in between
seasons and sideways
moving energy.

EAST

The element of
BIG WOOD
is associated with
the colour dark GREEN,
full grown plants,
flowers and seeds, the
season of spring and
outwards flowing energy.

The
CENTRE
is of the
EARTH
ELEMENT.

WEST

The element of
SMALL METAL
is associated with
WHITE, GOLD & SILVER
the season of autumn and
inward flowing energy.

NORTHEAST

The element of
SMALL EARTH
is associated with
the colour BEIGE, the
soil, the earth, anything
square, in between
seasons and horizontal
moving energy.

NORTH

The element of
WATER
is associated with
the colours BLACK & BLUE,
anything wavy in shape, the
season of winter and
meandering energy.

NORTHWEST

The element of
BIG METAL
is associated with
all METALLIC colours,
GOLD & SILVER,
the season of autumn and
inward flowing energy.

ABOUT MICHELE

Michele Castle has been a Feng Shui practitioner - consultant for more 2 decades. Trained by Master Raymond Lo, of Hong Kong at the Feng Shui Centre in Perth, Western Australia she has also studied with Dato Joey Yap and Lillian Too. Michele studies each year under various master's and is continually expanding her Feng Shui knowledge.

Michele taught Feng Shui, Chinese Astrology and Metaphysical studies for Asian studies unit at Curtin University.

Previously studying architectural drafting and interior design and working with interiors and renovations, on her own homes it was a natural progression to incorporate Feng Shui and metaphysical studies in her renovations. Applauded for her style, she was asked if she could do what she had been doing with her own homes to others. So, having a passion and dedication after further studies her first Feng Shui business, *Energise Life Feng Shui*, began, growing quickly and incorporating workshops, seminars and teaching it soon became known as *Complete Feng Shui*.

Michele conducts on-site Feng Shui consultations for residential and corporate clients, and as well as being an accredited teacher of Feng Shui, Michele is an author and public speaker. Michele works with residential homes, small to medium family businesses, larger corporations, developers, architects, interior designers, real estate agents, restaurants, cafes, day spas and retail stores. Michele specialises in one-on-one Chinese astrology and life path readings regarding health, love, and career opportunities.

For a business client, Michele can help with staff recruitment, assist with selecting the best location and orientation for business premises, improve the atmosphere and working environments and advise on business stationery such as letterheads and business cards.

For the residential client, Michele advises on how to improve health and harmony in the home, how to choose the best home as well as improve the chances of selling your present home, assist with identifying strengths in choosing suitable careers for the younger members of the family, guide older family members looking for a change in their current career path and how to alleviate difficulties children may be having with sleeping, studying and behaviour in general.

Michele is often in demand for speaking at events, local radio, interviewed on *Today Tonight, Better Life TV*, and is a regular on the WA television show *The Couch*, where she talks about all things Feng Shui. Michele has been recognised with local awards a winner of a Nifnex Influential 100 Awards, the New Emerging Business Award, Entrepreneur Award as well as Networking Award from the Soulful Awards Self Discovery Network on 2 occasions.

Michele teaches Feng Shui courses and workshops from beginners to practitioners alike, as well offering Feng Shui Retreats in Bali and now in WA where you can immerse yourself in 5 days of Feng Shui and Chinese Astrology; one of the world's most ancient arts and science of placement, to bring about balance between people and their environment. Michele also conducts on-site learning exercises at homes and for businesses, within Australia and overseas.

For those who have mastered the basics of Feng Shui and wish to continue their studies and share their knowledge with others, there are courses in 'Feng Shui as a Business', and the 'practitioners' course' where with practice and the correct training, one can learn to be a practitioner once mastering Feng Shui becoming an consultant. Once qualified, you have a responsibility to share the correct knowledge with your client. Choosing a Feng Shui consultant is like choosing a health care professional; you want someone who knows what they are doing, who understands your needs, and gives a reliable, knowledgeable advice.

Michele truly believes.

" Life is what our thoughts environment and energy make it".

"Change your environment and thoughts, change your life".

With the knowledge of Feng Shui, it can work to increase wealth, enhance health, and harmonise relationships.

Activating Peach Blossom Luck for Love

Feng Shui prescribes a simple method for helping single ladies and men find conjugal happiness. For those seriously looking for romance, love and marriage, you can activate your "Peach Blossom Luck!" Place your peach blossom animal in the correct location of your bedroom and this will activate peach blossom luck.

If you are a RAT, DRAGON or MONKEY, place a ROOSTER in the WEST of your bedroom.

If you are a RABBIT, SHEEP or BOAR, place a RAT in the NORTH of your bedroom.

N
W   E
S

If you are an OX, SNAKE or ROOSTER, place a HORSE in the SOUTH of your bedroom.

If you are a TIGER, HORSE or DOG, place a RABBIT in the EAST of your bedroom.

www.ingramcontent.com/pod-product-compliance
Lightning Source LLC
Chambersburg PA
CBHW040933050426
42334CB00050B/89